BEAVERS

BEAVERS

PETER MURRAY

THE CHILD'S WORLD

PHOTO RESEARCH

Charles Rotter/Gary Lopez Productions

PHOTO CREDITS

Tom & Pat Leeson: front cover,
back cover, 2, 10, 11, 13, 16, 19, 31
COMSTOCK/Townsend Dickinson: 6
Leonard Rue III: 9, 22, 25, 28
Len Rue Jr.: 14, 21, 27

Distributed to schools and libraries in the United States by
ENCYCLOPAEDIA BRITANNICA EDUCATIONAL CORP.
310 South Michigan Avenue
Chicago, Illinois 60604

Library of Congress Cataloging-in-Publication Data
Murray, Peter, 1952 Sept. 29-
Beavers / by Peter Murray.
p.   cm.
Summary: Introduces the physical characteristics,
behavior, and life cycle of beavers.
ISBN 0-89565-844-5
1. Beavers--Juvenile literature.   [1. Beavers.]   I. Title.
QL737.R632M87   1992   91-34732
599.32'32--dc20   CIP
                                                         AC

*For the beaver family at the Minnesota Zoo,
with thanks for their repeated demonstrations.*

One day you might be walking through the woods and come upon a big pond. You might wonder how such a pond got there, because a few weeks ago there was only a little creek running through the woods. Then you notice a huge mound of logs, sticks, mud, and leaves in the middle of the pond. At the far end there is a dam made of sticks and mud. Many of the trees nearby have been cut down, leaving pointy stumps with tooth marks on them. Beavers are watching you. The pile of sticks in the middle of the pond is their home.

Many animals build their own homes. Birds build nests. Foxes dig dens. Bees make hives. But only the beaver makes its own pond.

When a pair of beavers go off on their own to find a home, they look for a small stream with plenty of trees nearby. They cut down trees using their sharp teeth and drag them across the stream. They fill the gaps between the logs with smaller branches, leaves, and mud until the stream stops flowing. The water backs up behind the dam, making a pond where the beavers can begin construction of their new home.

Imagine trying to bite down a tree, even a small one. To a beaver, it is an everyday task. Beavers have large front teeth that slice through wood like sharp chisels. Their teeth have a hard orange coating that keeps them from chipping.

But chewing through trees can wear down even the strongest  teeth. Fortunately, a beaver's teeth keep growing as long as the animal is alive. They must use their teeth every day to keep them the right length. If a beaver stopped gnawing on trees, its teeth would soon grow too long and it could not close its mouth.

Once the beavers have created their own private pond, they start work on their home, or *lodge*. At first, the beaver lodge is a great mound of sticks and mud. When the pile is big enough, the beavers dig a hole under the surface of the water. Then they hollow out the pile. Usually beavers make two entrances to the lodge. One entrance leads to the dam, and the other leads to their winter food supply.

Beavers eat many different kinds of plants. In the warmer months, they dine on water plants, grasses, berries, and even mushrooms. But the beaver's favorite food is the moist bark of young aspen trees. They eat bark like we eat corn on the cob, turning a log to strip away the nutritious food.

If you are ever lucky enough to see one, you can always recognize a beaver by its large, flat, hairless tail. When swimming, a beaver uses its tail like a rudder to steer. It can also paddle with its tail to swim faster. A beaver's tail is useful for other things, too. When a beaver cuts down a tree, it uses its strong tail to balance itself. And when a beaver senses danger, it slaps its tail against the water so hard that it sounds like a gunshot. All the beavers take cover when they hear this sound.

Fall is the beavers' busiest time of the year. With winter coming, they must make sure that their home is strong enough to withstand the ice and cold. They put a new coat of mud on the lodge to insulate and strengthen it. They also reinforce the dam with new logs and branches.

Before winter comes, beavers must also put away enough food to last them until spring. A family of beavers can cut down over 100 trees for their winter food supply. They cut the trees into pieces and stick them into the mud at the bottom of the pond. Soon a large mass of twigs, branches, and logs reaches from the bottom of the pond all the way to the surface. This is called their *food raft*.

In winter the pond is frozen over and covered with a thick layer of snow. The beavers are safe and warm inside their lodge. When a beaver wants a snack, it leaves the lodge through the underwater tunnel and swims under the ice to the food raft. Beavers have special clear eyelids so they can see underwater with their eyes closed. They can stay underwater for over 15 minutes. The hungry beaver cuts a branch from the food raft and brings it back into the lodge to eat the bark.

In the spring, female beavers give birth to one to six baby beavers, called *kits*. The kits are born with their eyes open, their bodies covered with fur, and their big orange teeth ready for gnawing. Within a week, they are ready to take their first swim. The young beavers remain close to their mother. Sometimes they even climb up on her back or hold onto her tail for a free ride!

The young beavers stay with their parents for two years. When they are one year old, their mother gives birth to a second litter. As many as 12 beavers might be in the same family and live in the same lodge. If they need more room, the beavers pile more sticks and mud on top of the lodge, then hollow it out from the inside. Some large beaver families have lodges that are nearly as big as a small house!

The next spring, when yet another litter is born, it is time for the two-year-olds to leave home. One by one, they go upstream, or downstream, or off into the woods to search for a mate. Eventually, they will find a new place with running water and plenty of young aspen trees. There they will build their own dam, and their own lodge, and have their own litter of kits.

Beavers are found wherever there is clean running water, trees with nutritious bark, and room for them to build a home. Some people complain that beavers cut down valuable trees and cause flooding with their dams. But at the same time, beaver ponds create new places for fish, birds, and other creatures to live. And when beavers abandon their home, the dam soon breaks down and a new forest grows up in the rich soil that is left behind. Beavers have long been a part of the natural environment. We can enjoy them for their fascinating ways and for the important role they play in the cycle of nature.

THE CHILD'S WORLD
NATUREBOOKS

Wildlife Library

Alligators	Musk-oxen
Arctic Foxes	Octopuses
Bald Eagles	Owls
Beavers	Penguins
Birds	Polar Bears
Black Widows	Primates
Camels	Rattlesnakes
Cheetahs	Reptiles
Coyotes	Rhinoceroses
Dogs	Seals and Sea Lions
Dolphins	Sharks
Elephants	Snakes
Fish	Spiders
Giraffes	Tigers
Insects	Walruses
Kangaroos	Whales
Lions	Wildcats
Mammals	Wolves
Monarchs	Zebras

Space Library

Earth	The Moon
Mars	The Sun

Adventure Library

Glacier National Park	Yosemite
The Grand Canyon	Yellowstone National Park